THE REINVENTION OF THE HUMAN HAND

BOOKS BY PAUL VERMEERSCH

POETRY

The Reinvention of the Human Hand (2010)
Between the Walls (2005)
The Fat Kid (2002)
Burn (2000)

CHAPBOOKS

Widows and Orphans (2002)
What You Wish Wasn't True (1999)

AS EDITOR

The Al Purdy A-frame Anthology (2009)
The I.V. Lounge Reader (2001)

PAUL VERMEERSCH

THE REINVENTION
— *of the* —
HUMAN HAND

McClelland & Stewart

Library and Archives Canada Cataloguing in Publication

Vermeersch, Paul
The reinvention of the human hand / Paul Vermeersch.

Poems.
ISBN 978-0-7710-8743-1

I. Title.

PS8593.E74R44 2010   c811'.6   C2009-905155-9

Published simultaneously in the United States of America by McClelland & Stewart Ltd., P.O. Box 1030, Plattsburgh, New York 12901

Library of Congress Control Number: 2009935650

We acknowledge the financial support of the Government of Canada through the Book Publishing Industry Development Program and that of the Government of Ontario through the Ontario Media Development Corporation's Ontario Book Initiative. We further acknowledge the support of the Canada Council for the Arts and the Ontario Arts Council for our publishing program.

Typeset in Janson by M&S, Toronto
Printed and bound in Canada

This book is printed on acid-free paper that is 100% recycled, ancient-forest friendly (100% post-consumer waste).

McClelland & Stewart Ltd.
75 Sherbourne Street
Toronto, Ontario
M5A 2P9
www.mcclelland.com

1 2 3 4 5   14 13 12 11 10

For Chris Sloan

Finding out that the physical world was
not a theory or a feeling
was quite a shock for me.

— TONY HOAGLAND

CONTENTS

——

I

II

III

I

Their discovery has been a kind of homecoming, too.
Part of you has been here before, germinal, hidden.
A painted hand resting on the stone, a molecule,
a memory of muscled, brawling bulls entombed
deep within, their horns goring the darkness
locked in the rock of ages. These yellow ochre horses

were born too long before they could be anything
but horses, before they could be centaurs, before
they could be starships. Remember, these herds
are the same on these walls as they were in their fields,
the same as they are in your mind. Listen.
Their hoof beats trampling this ancestral earth

are still the drums that drive the song in your blood,
the abiding chant of the hundred billion dead
who came before you. Their distant voices vanished
into your voice, deepening it. Their song the song
that's been snarled in your heart – breaking it,
trying to pound its way free – for your entire life.

A SCORPION IN ALCOHOL

Fifteen years in isopropyl alcohol
has burned the dull, brownish
pigment from its carapace,

but still you keep it, dead and pale,
in your kitchen, as a keepsake
of the time that you, too, almost died.

Or so you thought, until the Bahamian
graveshift doctor laughed
at the harmless juvenile specimen you brought him,

the one you found crawling on your nightie
after a midnight row of pinpricks,
bathroom lights and stifled screams.

This tiny, primal question mark
curled up, lifeless, in its jar
once had the strength

to sink a small, dark drop of apprehension
beneath your skin – a venom so subtle, it lingers
and threatens to ruin you still.

ODE TO *AMOEBA PROTEUS*

Little one, you have mastered the arts of taking
and giving. Even the tiniest crumb you take
with the whole of yourself, enveloping it,
creating a hollow place inside of you
to keep it hidden, to keep yours, until that place
is empty again, and it collapses in upon itself,
and the need to fill it returns, and you take.

But when you give, little one, there is no saint
or saviour who can match your generosity.
Only you can give yourself twice, each
to a different future, each from a single past.
I even believed it was possible, once, to give and take
the way you do, when the world seemed made of knives,
and all I wanted was flesh, and all I felt was want.

BOSCH LANDSCAPE 2010

for Stuart Ross

Discovered during the restoration
of Saint John's cathedral, it depicts
six hills on fire and their reflections
in the eyes of spooked horses. The sky
is smoke. The trees beyond the town
are smoke, their branches like white hands
clamouring for air, leafless, impotent.

Strange creatures, bizarre chimeras
flee the disaster and flood the square,
startling the townspeople. The faces
of the dispossessed are doubled in a tower
of mirrors: cod-face and rabbit-face,
blackbird-face and owl. Coin-sides
to one another, holding closed books.

A throng of ice skaters with outsized ears
are racing around a ruined, wooden church.
They play lutes made of mussel shells
and toss golden keys into a river of pitch.
It's a parable of corruption, the experts say,
and a warning against the decline of reason.
Hell on Earth, they say, is ignorance.

The fires of ignorance, Bosch says, they say,
are burning all around us, and their smoke
conceals the corruption. They cannot explain,
however, the significance of the lemurs

riding the horses, or the warthog driving
the blue convertible Eldorado, or why
the statue of Charles Darwin holds a knife.

They are stumped by the man in boxing gloves,
his face tattooed with mysterious symbols.
They are flummoxed by the haloed saints
and angels tearing panels from the belly
of a space shuttle hurtling wildly Earthward.
The priests and critics just gape in wonder
with painted flames mirrored in their eyes.

HANDS

I dreamt of finger bones
as thick as treesnakes,
of hands that possessed
a fierce, primeval strength,
and I awoke with swollen
knuckles, as though I had
smashed them hard against stone.

But my bed was soft and my back
ached from the excess of comfort.
Each night, the dreams grew worse.
I saw, severed from their body,
the heavy, black hands
of a mountain silverback.
It felt like wires tightening
around my wrists as I slept.

Dogs in the city. Unwanted, they circle the heart.
These things happen: a young dog turned away
from its master's house will pine at the gate
for a while, certain there has been some mistake,
but there's no mistake. Its wounded howling
only reveals the clean inertia of its love.

Whatever moves it – hunger, thirst, or just
the need to be far from that place – moves it
through the always empty streets, where the things
it eats and drinks make it sick, and where a damp chill
begins to penetrate its coat, deranging its howl
with a cough when it finally touches the skin.

Older dogs answer it, their howls from the fringe
beyond the heart. It's a sound of garbled savagery
and resignation. These creatures, once the helpmates
of their houses, now snap and froth and abhor the living.
The young dog listens – it is my love for you, my love –
and soon it will leave to join with the others.

ALTARPIECE WITH FALSE TEETH AND PARKINSON'S DISEASE

for Margaret Vermeersch and Leopold "Paul" Couvreur in memoriam

1 *Carousel*

In the first panel, blond celestial choirboys in glorious
white nightshirts, with shining diadems of light
above their heads, all turn in disgust from the carousel
of blackened goats, bloated pigs and wolves in iron helmets.
A fish lies rotting in the grass. Everywhere people
are naked and writhing. There is no comfort for them.

For some, a long life means a slow death. For Margaret
and Leopold, it begins before they're born, upwind
of German mustard gas, safe in the ochre haylofts
of the Flemish Masters, where those who do not die
too quickly might live long enough to pass on family
names, and because they are fertile and haven't sagged
into their graves, they copulate amidst exploding shells
and give birth to the next generation of the European doomed.

2 *Slaughterhouse*

In the centre panel, a stunned cow stands in the slaughterhouse
bleeding from its forehead. Like the young century,
it refuses to go down with the hammerstrike and requires
a second, more devastating blow. Behind it, hanged
alongside a skinless lamb, is a row of tiny, blindfolded men
above a feeding trough bursting with Christ's thorn.

Sometimes the children of war, like embers, ignite
new conflagrations when the waters of old conquests
subside. So Margaret and Leopold, born of war, are married
to the tune of the "Colonel Bogey March." Their country,
once again a sea of muck, is overrun by the same old foes
and their furious young. And who's that in the shadows?
A grotesque little imp in a beige tunic and jodhpurs
milking the infected, swollen udder of the cow!

Then, in the final panel, Leopold's pink and white dentures
hover in the sky above the North Sea's surging coastline –
could it be a lost Magritte? – while Margaret stands
at the crest of a majestic cliff, clutching a brown jug
marked with a cross. On her face, an expression of utmost
gravitas as she blesses the flying teeth with a sprinkle of water.

Older now, less steady, wracked with tremors. Every time
his teeth drop to his lap, he offers a helpless little shrug
and a smile. What can it mean to Leopold to be the boilerplate
man of his era, a decent man besieged by war and illness, and yet
in love? And Margaret? The long-suffering wife, faithful and faithful,
and still in love? Such extraordinary ordinariness! Come lay your
sacrifices here! Come lay your history, the practised extravagance
of your art, the buried crimes of your people, lay them here.

And be humbled.

THE SADNESS WILL LAST FOREVER

after Vincent Van Gogh

There is no blue
without yellow and without orange.
My room is blue, and in it the green chairs
are arranged at odd angles. Sometimes I can almost bear it.

People eat potatoes.
The skull clenches its burning
cigarette. All my friends look bored. I have
played hell somewhat with the truthfulness of the colours.

My shoes are worn.
I see drawings and pictures
in the poorest of huts and the dirtiest of corners.
My brother sends me money. Sometimes I can almost bear it.

My friend was a genius.
His ego and his syphilis made him
unreasonable. The best way to know life is to love
many things. These flowers are royal purple and tangerine.

Great things are done
by a series of small things brought together.
Coal-black crows erupt from the canary-coloured wheat.
My brother will be buried at my side. The sadness will last forever.

TWENTY-ONE DAYS WITH A BABOON HEART

for Baby Fae

Since our dawning in the Great Rift Valley
they have been our primordial reflections,
dog-faced shadows at the edge of our world.

Where we formed a circle
against the snarling cosmos,
they formed their circle beyond us, farther still.

When we reached out in their direction,
they reached back with long, slender hands
much stronger than our own.

None of us who see their yawning mouths
fail to regard them as the Lion People.
They face and fight and fear what we cannot know.

When one of their hearts was fixed inside
an infant girl, in Orwell's year, how long
do you suppose she survived with their terror?

The last of the ice cap finally splinters like a tray
of ice cubes cracked into a pail,
and the wooden workshop floor buckles into the ice cold
water and begins to sink. Slowly
at first, bottle-bobbing in the black and white
ice-choked swells, then slipping deeper
as it fills, until its buoyant trash
spills out – nutcracker, skin horse, and baby doll –
bubbled up and scattered all about, each
in a dead-man's float, before the whole picture is swallowed.

As the surface calms itself, the candy-coloured spires
of the workshop plunge downward
through the ever-darkening green, trailing
its inventory of rewards, its thousand years of legend,
its blackmail paid in chores and the niceness
of the nice. Yes, Virginia,
there is a Greenland shark, with parasites
trailing from its blighted eyes,
nosing through the wrecked and lightless halls of Christmas
deep beneath the vanished ice.

Which is more alive? A tiger at its kill,
or a child's plush tiger, or a child's plush tiger
in a storybook, or an illustration
of a child's plush tiger in a storybook?

Why, I am, of course, says the illustration
of a child's plush tiger in a storybook.

Can one improve on the love of Geppetto?
Can one succeed where the Great Oz failed?
Which is more alive? A heart that aches
and races, or an artificial heart?

They are equal, says the little
wooden man. *They are equal.*

APE

for Koko
and for Michael in memoriam

I

Ape born in Frisco, born out of darkness of mountain
        forests, out of rain that doesn't fall, but hovers.
Come, Ape, out of bushmeat trade and war zone, out of
        coffee and tea for human need.
Come out of blood diamond, come out of strip mine, out
        of pit viper and mosquito, out of tick.
Ape who lives in Woodside, Ape who rides in Honda,
        who wears red sweater. Come speak.
Ape of legend, come. Out of colonial science, out of Bible,
        come monster of Skull Island, of Original Sin, of
        City of Gold, come take this kitten to your breast
        and speak of love unconditional, Earthmotherhood.
What did the old men make of you, Ape, when they drew
        their Victorian cartoon, when they posed for their
        daguerreotype holding your scalp? Teeth of the
        meat-eater? Murderer's hands? Bush devil?
        Gargoyle? Proof?
Come Morning Star, come Adversary, daughter of the East.
        Come beast-thing, come witch, child of the Nephilim,
        giant in the Earth, come demonstrate the egg-shell
        gentleness of your strength.
And what did the young men make of you when they came
        with their machete genocide, radiating smoke?
They made you Lamb of the wilderness, one animal's breath

at the centre of the green and white day. Hush-a-bye,
hidden, quiet with your kind on the unclimbed slopes.
There, in shadow, in the hovering rain, the family almost stirs.

2

Ape! Ape! We thought you were gone! We thought you
      were gone into the book. We thought the damp
      black covers of untreated hide had closed around
      you forever.
Gone into the Book of Sasquatch. There were reports.
      There were sightings.
Gone into the Book of Yeti. There were such bloodcurdling
      cries in the highlands, footprints that vanished under
      the snow falling in the pass. It left us cold.
Ape, we thought you were gone. It was aboard the hulking
      wooden ships of Empire that you left us.
It was locked inside the gilded wagons of the circus, as tin
      calliopes whistled notes of sweltering air, that at last
      you left us.
We thought you were gone into shopping cart, into camera,
      into cake. We thought you were gone, Ape, into a
      discount mall display window for twenty-seven years
      without soil or mountain, without privilege or credit.
Ape, we feared, as the valleys emptied, as the land broke into
      atolls and everything was distant, as the beaches
      crumbled and the sea was left unreachable, Ape,
      we feared the worst.
Stories make things closer. Come now, Ape, and speak.
      There are stories of a boy who, by great misfortune,
      fell into your powerful care, who lived with you
      among the bamboo and lianas, and who learned,
      as well, to be Ape.
Tell us, Ape. Are the stories true? Was he everything that
      might make us proud?
Or did he shame us with his nakedness?

3

Ape of helicopter crash and gunboat, Kalashnikov foundling
in the burning brush, snatched by crate, smuggled by
truck, why be silent now?
Come now, Ape, out of black bazaar, out of bamboo cage on
meat-stained table, smelling of gasoline in the insect-
heavy air, come hoot the low, open vowel of your
name.
Ape of camera crew and cutting room, flickering between
solid shafts of tree trunk and weightless shafts of
light, come speak like this: *flickering, tree, light,*
and you will conjure the world of Ape.
We are listening. Across this forest floor darkened by limbs
crowded with birds, through the colliding sound waves
of their love songs and alarms, come speak.
Tell us, Ape, in your own words, why did the young men
come to the forest?
Squash meat gorilla. Mouth tooth.
And how did it sound to Ape?
Cry, sharp-noise loud!
And how did they look to Ape?
Bad think-trouble look-face.
And what has become of Ape's mother?
Cut/neck, lip (girl) hole.
Come now, Ape, out of landmine and hand grenade, out of
the smouldering charcoal fires of Virunga. Downriver
upon the deep arteries of the Congo, upon aluminum
wings across the sea, come speak to us.
Speak to us, Ape, in research-centre sanctuaries with hoseable
linoleum floors. Come speak to us from government-
funded genome projects, on glass slides of blood, from

the ancient common darkness inside cells, come speak
to us, please, in the language of Ape.
Come quick. Come now. The family is gathering.

The doctors will tell you the attraction
is mainly about the transformation,
the Freudian super-puberty of muscle and hair,
the id unleashed, the fantasy of becoming
something else, the other primal self, a form
in which the darker appetites of man,
unchecked by reason, can be fulfilled without
remorse or thoughts of consequence,
that lust is always lust whether born
in the animal mouth or in the belly or the groin.

But the boys who envy werewolves know
that isn't it at all. It's not about wishing
to be something else, even if there are
certain rewards that come with sharper teeth
and claws, with a powerful grip applied
to the trachea of one's enemy, how
the tissue of the throat must yield,
must open to the bone-deep intent
of the hand. It would be so much better
than becoming an actual school shooter.

Because who knows where anyone gets
the guns or the last-straw desperation?
And that act, too, requires a certain
transformation, a step away from who
you are, and that's really not the point.
The boys who envy werewolves do not
want to change. They only want the freedom
to be the monsters they know they are,

harbingers of the justice that seethes
inside them, the storm of bile unleashed,

the wage of bruises earned, long overdue.
No metamorphosis, but freedom
to be the howling in their earliest minds
broke loose, the animal ideas that gnaw
and scrape forever at the panels of bone
behind their faces. Our little brothers,
wild things in their beds of cartoon sleep,
ever silent about their broken fingers,
biding their time without word or trouble,
animal ideas pacing in their rooms of skin.

II

I AM HAPPY TO LIVE IN AN AGE OF PLENTY

There are more non-prescription painkillers now
than when most of us had jobs that were strenuous
or fatal. Our muscles tightened and frayed like ropes
that hoist pianos; our knuckles swelled and throbbed in time
with the weather, all against the acetaminophen tide.

And now we have more rounds of ammunition
than when most of us, for no better reason
than necessity, hunted for our meat, so many rounds
of ammunition, no meat can outrun the volume of lead
that we have loaded, cocked and aimed against its escape.

And there are far more children now than when we lived
in the desert and suffered from such loneliness we sang
our psalms to the empty sky for a little bit of company,
so many children born, filled with painkillers and meat,
there is now one child, they say, for every round of ammunition.

BASIC INSTRUCTIONS FOR ANAESTHESIA

I

Life consumes life. Even the hardest part
of you will weaken. The tooth will rot.
It must be removed or lived with. So start
with laughing gas. The idea is not
to feel the instruments loosening the root,
or the drill whirring its way into the bedrock
of gum and bone. The idea is to forget
the ache, to inhale the gas through a plastic
nozzle placed over the nose as the masked
dentist scrapes with his hook, extracts
the dead tissue, the blackened tooth.
Even the hardest part of you will weaken.
It must be removed or lived with.
The idea is not to feel. The idea is to forget.

2

Whiskey does the trick. Enough of it
can knock you out cold while the medic
cuts clean through your leg, if that's
what you need. Where the shin is twisted,
where the bone protrudes, there's something best
forgotten: birthdays turned necrotic,
a marriage, a festering assault.
Life consumes life. Like spoilt flesh, a thought
becomes infected, incurable. It must
be removed or lived with. Whiskey does the trick.
Even the hardest part of you will weaken.
Shattered bones encase the lump of heart.
Everything desperately wants to be felt.
But the idea is not to feel. The idea is to forget.

His irate youth lingers in the air. It clings
to his skin like the scent of a killed child,
a better twin whose brilliant memory persists
outside some locked and unlit box. It shines
right in his eyes, weakening and aging him.
With yesterday's rage dressed in yesterday's clothes,
he kneels beside a friend's grave, crying
Punk is dead! Punk is dead! He claws
at the grass, frantic for the aimless, ear-splitting
riffs of his former strength. He is so angry now
about Ma Bell's arrogance, about the transmission
in his eight-year-old Impala, about knowing so much
about death. He has forgotten how to feel it,
that proud, scattergun hatred: *disco, Nazis, dad.*

PRAYER TO A SAINT

Cross yourself, if you're the type, struck
dumb from your dumb horse, blinded, drunk

on visions of pale bombs falling, a sinner
impaled on the spear of a cherub.

Don't be afraid. They don't burn people
for hearing the voices, not anymore.

SMOKE

I

As small as I was, before my hair ever darkened,
when I was still a flash of white, my platinum locks,
my baby teeth, the perfect sclera that had never shown
blood vessels already burrowing like pinworms
into some distant morning's hangover, some rage
at grown-up failures, when I was still that flawless,
that twenty-four-carat pure, I knew it was you
who came into our house and weakened my father's heart,
who choked my mother's laugh into a cracked and arid rasp.
I saw you loitering in our kitchen, clinging to our windows,
wearing your crude perfume, when in my nightmares
you were always hiding in the closet, or under the bed,
or curled up like a polyp in the dog's nostril, waiting
to explode. You lived with us. You touched everything.

We met again when I was sweet sixteen, you so neat
and slim in your white slip, and me sliding, glass by glass,
into my first drunk. At night in a friend's backyard
fifteen years ago, the fire-lit trees spread their branches
into darkness. The stars above them seemed a little nervous
when they twinkled. The chatter was coming unravelled;
voices walked across the lawn without their mouths,
saying words like "punk" and "fuck" and "faggot,"
words without targets, exempt from meaning, so that
the edges peeled away from every sound, every memory.
When someone refused to kiss you, you came to me,
surprised at how much I'd grown – taller, darker –
and though you hadn't changed, I wasn't frightened.
I brought you to my mouth and breathed you in all night.

1 *Boy*

In the cradle's green canopy an animal
with the piercing cry of a human child
moves with unsettling swiftness through
the highest branches. Until it is killed.

The next is no different. Ditto the next.
Changes come only imperceptibly, or
at intervals, monstrously, until it climbs
down from the leaves to be a boy in the grass.

And now he stands, growing taller,
and trains his eye on the horizon
where greater beasts eat and are eaten.

He is terrified of their shapes that change
with the light, but he is armed with new tools,
and he aims to be their king.

Mother was rock and tree to the boy.
She was river and rain. He killed
the most beautiful animal for her
and wore it on his back like a second body.

When she would not rise or follow,
she was not there. He could scour
the entire world with a flaming torch
in the thick fog of dawn but never find her.

He wants to see her rise again like the sun,
shedding her light on all visible things,
coaxing fresh life, pink and silver,
from the rivers, but she will not rise.

3 *Tongue*

The boy stands upright and naked in the dawn,
hungry in the onslaught of photons, pronouncing
his word for the world, flexing his tongue,
the only muscle that knows, that names.

His tongue says: *Mother. Milk. Meat.*
His tongue says: *Maggot.*
His tongue says: *Morte. Muerte. Morbid. Mort.*
His tongue says: *More.*

Perhaps another organ says: *The sun is hot,*
seek shade. The belly is empty, but fire
is technology, child, and life is fleeting,
so bury her with marshmallow flowers.

He hears the words inside himself, so he obeys
and digs a fragrant grave for her.
He is, unto himself, an undiscovered science.
Horses do not pull the sun across the sky.

4 River

He grumbles to himself about his emptiness,
but he already knows how to push
a broken stick through a warm heart,
how to unlock blood with a stone.

And there is a river that bends, and where it bends
there is a tree of ripe fruit, and where
there's fruit, he celebrates. Shake an apricot
from a bough or spear a fish, it's the same celebration.

And so the river passes over the round stones.
And so the water passes out of sight.
And so the fruit will someday pass with the fish
into the unseen country of water and mothers.

5 *Wolf*

And the wolf, as dawn breaks into the full
light of day, is a staring contest for the boy.
And the wolf pack is a laceration.

And the wolf's ancestor, with its long-gone
yellow eyes, is a laceration now forgotten
everywhere but in the mud that hides

its long white bones. Once they loved and hated
the way men do, with all they have, and they had gazes, too,
that seized upon the world like heart attacks.

But soon the pack will be no match for the boy
and his fire, his sticks and stones, his names
for things, and they will turn their heads

away from him, conceding their defeat, and he
will get on with the business of killing things
in the glorious absence of gods.

I

Will it go unnoticed, the human race in its widowhood,
its trophy wife gone? The operatic ending of Ingrid,
last of the blondes. Diaphanous mother, cancerous wife,
last, lost and forgotten among the legions of bottled
impostors. Anonymous in her death, in her row house,
lullabyed by the passing of ancestors, gods of thunder,
their *–sons* and *-dötters*, great warriors and hustlers
of golden sex in glossy print. Oh, don't forget the healers
on battlefields, and the tyrants, and the barbarians,
beloved for their uncommon locks. Golden Ingrid,
before the Valkyries abduct you to Valhalla,
afterworld of the blonde, will you weave your curls
into keychains for keepsakes? Will you secretly bleach
your children's hair to ensure their passage after you?

2

Or will your birth be multinational, Ingrid, co-opted
by governments and syndicates? Will you become
their Golden Child, their Chosen One, their brand?
The paparazzi will take your picture. There will be stories
of your first steps and all your steps thereafter. Ingrid,
you will be invited to galas, inaugurations, the moon.
Oh, they'll crowd around you on the moon mourning
the cruelty of evolution, that anything so fair cannot
endure. And they will gather around your bed to cover
your passing – the human family diminished, the bright
noon sunlight of the genome extinguished – as geneticists
bank samples of your blood, your tears, your hair, your
warm electroplated hair that will continue to grow
for a day or two, the legends will say, even after you're gone.

after Jan Asselyn, circa 1650

On the subway platform, the young woman huddles
her two children behind the hem of her milk-white coat.
It's a dangerous world – maybe bloodthirsty hounds
are already prowling through Ossington Station.
Maybe evil men have been released into society again.
Distant automobiles might already be speeding toward
the intersection she will need to cross with her kids
later this afternoon – and she must keep them safe.
She is like Asselyn's *The Threatened Swan*
in the Rijksmuseum – beautiful, but more so from a distance.

Like the swan, she knows she is the guardian of a possible
future contained within a clutch of fragile eggs, and she too
has jet black eyes that would like to love the whole world
all at once, but can't, can't because a hound, mad with hunger,
has come down from the bald-pate hills to the North.
Approaching by water, it sees the brittle shells packed
with unassembled life. To the hound they are time capsules,
a chance to wrest the future from its nesting place and feed,
so the threatened swan splays her black feet in the wet mud
and drums her milk-white wings against the seventeenth-century sky.

In the tunnel beneath the city, the train's whistle deafens mice
that have never seen the sky. The oncoming light spreads
over mildewed walls like a dingy sun rising sideways
through greasy, tattered clouds. That's when her three-year-old
son tears away from her coat and bolts for the yellow line.
Pushing her daughter to the wall, she thrashes after him.

The deaf mice scramble as the whistle blasts its shockwave
and the iron floor shakes. That's when she truly becomes the swan –
her white feathers scatter, her voice breaks like a heavy chain
swinging through a slate wall. First it creaks . . . and then it shatters.

What melody, what chorus? Something *mezzo-*
piano downloaded from a prenatal
memory, something soft, but not
too soft, so he will know that it's his mother
calling, the ringtone programmed
with the first song he remembers ever
hearing on the radio – it is June, and the backyard
is filled with the kind of light that burns,
and there are faded lawn chairs that one day
will be folded away forever, when his mother calls.

And when his oldest friend calls, his phone
repeats an inside joke from years ago,
an innuendo of savage cruelty directed
at a long-forgotten classmate, but the joke remains
hilarious, to them and no one else. You see,
this is how he privately assigns significance
to the people in his life. Each ringtone
becomes the herald. So when his
girlfriend calls, the song that plays gently
reminds him how much better the sex used to be.

Now when his older brother calls, there is a silence
as the phone shakes fearfully in his pocket,
a silence like his brother kept as violent
assailants surrounded him on the white pea-gravel
to press his face into the chain-link –
it shakes once for his buried resentment
and twice for his hatred of sports;
it shakes again for his deviated septum and again

and again and again for the beloved secret tree fort
constantly being vandalized inside him.

And for his father, should it be his father's music
from the hit parade of cigarettes and hideous
suits? Or should it be the sound of a man
coming home from work, the engine dying
in sputters and the *chunck* of the car door,
and then the sound of him lifting his boy
above his head and spinning him
all around the living room like a helicopter
without ever saying a word because
his world is that important and unknowable?

PROSTHETIC LEG IN STORAGE

The hickory thigh varnished to a gloss
above the creaking metal knee
feels nothing, not the tarnished brass
thumbtack pushed into its grain,
a souvenir of aches and pains now lost
except in thoughts of how they stung.

With a cane to match, black-lacquered oak
topped with copper, his every stride
was another dormant pratfall, another joke
in the offing, but he could still be proud
of the craftsmanship it took
to make three clicks across the kitchen floor.

Those lopsided steps took their toll
on his good leg, grown old
with a cane's strange tripod stance,
until a set of wheels were rolled
beneath the undestroyed limb, and a stillness
tamed the bones marooned forever in their chair.

shows a veiny, red disc resembling single strands of Spanish
moss against a blood-orange tropical moon, or the surface
of a smouldering volcanic planet showered with forked
and ruby-coloured lightning. But that's only if the eye is healthy.
Macular degeneration looks like black bubbles melting the middle
of the world, while glaucoma eats away at vision's edges
and works its way inward, eating until there's nothing left
to look at but the narrowing aperture of what's right in front
of your slowly disappearing nose. No one ever wants to go
blind. Even when they die, they want their eyes to continue
seeing something. They want to believe the last brilliantly
beautiful thing, however terrifying or mild, that they will ever see
in their priceless, suddenly finished lives will be captured,
immortalized like an image on film. They want death
to come on like shutter speed – *snap!* And what remains?
The face of your true killer superimposed on the blood-orange moon
or your loved ones finally gathered on a planet swarmed by firestorms.

III

They have achieved the size and shape
of empty mouths. They are millions
of wild green tongues. They are blue
poison darts and ripe strawberries. Tongues,
bull and leopard, striped and pitted,
with scarlet eyes, humble, medicinal,
wart-studded tongues, all singing
mud-covered notes wrapped in rubber.

They sound like broken ukulele strings,
like a swampful of banjos plucking, or maybe
a deep, guttural bogsong – and they sound
their long-drawn-out trills that buzz
like small electric motors in the treetops.
All the voices that strum and belch,
that come in bubbles from the muck
of the early Devonian, and the tortured
among them that scream like we scream.

Through the dark, end-Permian nights they sang
while the oceans slept through the final
dying of the trilobites, the same choir
that lullabyed diplodocus into its grave,
and smilodon, and thylacine, and dodo.
And still they sing, though not for us,
their ancestors' mantra: *I am here, I am here.*
But it's getting hot, and it's getting late.
The old singers are taxed and spent,
and their songs will fall hushed before sunrise.

IN JOSEPH MERRICK'S LONDON

My body, like this city, boomed and sprawled.
The steam engine, with its lathe and spinning mule,
brought thousands from the counties, but the city
couldn't hold them all, and so the city bulged
wild and gross about its core. And so my body bulged
from the strain of its own revolution, but what
the mechanism was that drove the change, I cannot fathom.

This right arm, no longer *my* right arm, lost its battle
and swelled into a slum. It doesn't work. It's sore.
The change happened young. First the skin rebelled,
and then the bones, then all. I cut my crooked teeth
in sideshows, but soon I was under my own big top,
my skull. In back of shops, in back streets,
behind the curtain wall, here's what's in store:

I am the cobblestones come loose beneath your feet
that break your stride. I am the unexpected fall.
I am the rubble of the sacred: God's likeness smashed
in mankind's fragile glass. I am the prayer deflected.
I am the lately crippled, waking up among the crippled,
bleary-eyed, into his new crippled life. And worse, I am
my young stepmother's deficit of love when I required more.

THE MARRIAGE OF THE NUCLEI

Something borrowed in the blood,
a neighbour's tools, a ladder,
things you've kept too long
to ever give back, cups
of sugar in the blood, scissors
to snip the tips off things.

Something blue in the reflection,
a different quality of light, a new eye
unlike the parents' eyes,
or an inward blue
that outlines the organs against the skin
as though backlit.

Something old, older maybe than a blood-fat tick
in amber,
or the twisted protein chains inside
the drop of life it swallowed,
a flaw in the flaw in the way
this story was repeated was repeated was.

What you love most is made this way,
little face like your face
when it was little. And what you hate
is made this way, too,
something very wrong with the face,
something new.

DOGSTAR

for Laika

The orbit of this satellite
tightens like a tether on a pole.

From here, cities look like psoriasis,
like mange on a belly.

I'm just a mongrel bitch
from the alleys of Moscow.

Now I see mountain ranges,
the texture of nipples, stretched out.

And all below the treeline, trees.
Like fur . . . with fleas.

The whole thing is the occluded
blue iris of a beautiful husky.

The whole thing
is a ball.

They will build a statue for me,
and I will be Queen of all the Russians.

I can destroy them all from here
with my eyes.

LOVE AS AN ARGUMENT IN THEORETICAL PHYSICS

We have our backs to the city, ignoring its insistence
that everything is familiar to us, that we have already seen
this street, this building, that we know the world
around us, its deep crevasses into which our past selves
have fallen, that what we're feeling we have already
felt, time and again. We could remind it, "But each time
is different." We too could insist, but that would mean
acknowledging its claims that everything repeats itself,
that all this has happened before, that all this, too,
could happen again. The tall white building at the corner
of Bloor and Balmuto was already built in another age.
Someday, it will be destroyed. Someday, it will be built again.

A GLASS EYE FINDS ITS PURPOSE

I came in a bottle, a prize like the worm
in the mezcal you swallowed
in lieu of an apology. Isn't it lovely
how I complement your fragile face?

My gold-flecked chestnut iris is
a perfect match to your
gold-flecked chestnut iris, but
I fail to redden when your mood flags,

or when the nervous field-mouse beating
of your heart makes sleep impossible,
or when drinking deepens it
and you awake a little damaged.

I know I'm no great help. I fail to flinch
at the fist that brought me here, raised
in your blind periphery. I fail to see
how I can be of any use to you except

as a decoy . . . a fake to draw away
his jabs, his right hooks and uppercuts,
to blur his wild uneven blows, to lure
your twin ballistic voices, the slurred

epithets you swap, like broken teeth
spat against a wall, to finally bring
the rising, untreatable fever of your love
into the umbra where everything's equal.

THE REINVENTION OF THE HUMAN HAND

for Annette

Ten years after the twin furies
of poor visibility and clouded
judgment curled their foggy
fingers under the chrome and
plastic bumper of her suv
and rolled it half a dozen times
down a stretch of country road,
the process is almost complete.

The reinvention of the human hand
takes time. The failed attempts:
a forked stick, a dog's mouth, a monkey's paw.
But now electric substitutes for nerves
implanted in her skin replace
the once-sparking tresses of her brain,
long since cropped at the neck,
locking her a decade in the skull's tower.

But now we see her close her fingers
around a water glass and raise it
to her lips. There is a quenching here
of something more than thirst, more
than the body's clumsy struggle for survival,
a simple need that now seems animal
compared to others: the need to brush
a strand of hair from one's own face,

the need to catch a falling knife
or hold a pen and write one's name,
the need to run one's fingers over skin
and be reminded how the body only
acts on the mind's behalf, and most of all
the need, now that it's completely understood,
to move the lifeless objects of this world
that cannot move themselves.

HE CONSIDERS THE POSSIBILITY THAT NONE OF THIS IS REAL

My cave and Plato's cave are not so different, really.
We're all imprisoned here. None of this is real.
The bats rouse at dusk and the commotion of shadows
tells a story of wakefulness and departure, a story
of the return from the hunt and the nursing of the young.
I admire its simplicity, though I could never play a part
in such a tale. I inhabit a man-made world, and it needs me.

I, too, can move the dark. Tonight I practise casting
my signature against the walls, flapping my hands
in the lamplight, passing the quiet hours on a night
with no emergency, a silent lacuna
in the ongoing disaster. But even I succumb sometimes
to the boredom of tranquility. I straighten my mask
in the bathroom, brush the garlicky crumbs from my lap.

At times like this I wish the cave itself was just some pale
invention of an idle mind, that the true world lay just outside,
unthinkable in its colours, in its shapes and in its weight,
in the wonders that it holds and in the wonders that refuse to be held,
that I could step this moment from the pages of my own life story
to be thrilled and disappointed by a life with richer blood
than the thin black ink to which I've grown accustomed.

The crash site sparks with small fires
that fail to penetrate the scenery. All
your crew is out of health. The enemy
is everywhere. This is the first level.
This is where your life begins.

Now press the green button. Now find your gun. Now move
with your left-hand control. You have three men
to start with. You are alone. Remember,
this is only the beginning. You don't know
anything yet. Shoot with X. Use O to escape.

Hand-like, a crab, joints clicking, enfolds
your head like a gasmask. It knows
what you have never known, that you are made
of light. It wants you. Or it wants you to try
to reach the next level before your life is gone.

THREE ANTHROPOMORPHIC STUDIES

for Mel Blanc

I *Duck Season*

It's not for lack of effort I'm no hero.
Pig-man, you've known me long enough.
In ancient Sherwood's fertile woodland,
you were the modest cleric I schooled
in the arts of battle – the dodge and thrust
of justice, the parry and spin of valour –
and you've been my loyal servant ever since.
In Victoria's England we matched our wits
against mankind's depravity . . . and lost,
or prevailed . . . who can remember anymore?
Lives and deeds long gone, they seem unreal.

My life, however, has not always been
so honourable. I was born a lunatic,
a wanton little mallard, and my greed
was want to get the best of me. I've swindled
as often as I've saved, stolen everything
I've offered up as alms, and it gets worse.
Four hundred years ago, I sold a man
the bright, blue button of a happier, easier life,
and a red button I warned him not to push.

Well, he pushed it, and that was the end of us . . .
that time, at least. There have been so many
endings, I've lost count. So many rifles
pointed at my skull, their triggers squeezed

when I demanded mercy, so many boomeranged
conspiracies, grasps at wealth and power turned
backward, fatal. In truth, I've been a coward,
but a greedy coward, and I've paid for it.

Little of my original insanity remains.
Memories come mixed with unsettling
visions: trusted friends in violent rage,
they threaten me with glinting,
blackened weapons, then recoil
in disgust from my spasms. Worst
is when I see your face among them,
altered in its anger, younger, less your own.

There are times I fear it's never truly over,
my old psychosis, duck season, my bald
Achilles' heel, though I know the world
has other plans for me, the foolish world!
It's peaceful now, a pool of glassy blue,
but forces are gathering to shatter it.
The pond cannot defend against the stone,
nor can the grass hold back the wind.
By army, or by asteroid, everything will end.

And who has put their faith in us,
a pair of battle-weary soldiers past their prime,
the last defenders of the Earth,
or mere pretenders to the role? Oh reckless Earth!
Today is far too quiet, and it troubles me.
I warm the coffee and I watch the screens.
Flying cars shimmer in the sunrise below us,
and the satellites are pulling at the seas.

Today, Roadrunner, like every day,
the clouds in our sky, these pencil-thin
translucent shapes, are sparse
and a little too evenly spaced, and rain
to moisten my parched and cracking lips
is a little too much to hope for.

Instead of rain today, perhaps an anvil
will fall. How heavy the burden
that drives me like a nail into the earth!
How painful the music in my bones,
like hollow reeds, when I emerge, a shaggy
brown accordion from the staggering blow.

And today, the saguaros are too green
for the angular, never-setting sun.
The cacti mock me: *Incompetent trickster!*
Quixotic fool! And they mark their spines
with the many names of my weaknesses:
appetite, cowardice, neurosis, the knot
in my stomach when the rocky ledge
suddenly gives way beneath my feet.
I ignore their jibes – how could they know
I've read all the German thinkers
in German, the French in French?

Some days, I'd gladly surrender
my little black heart, though maybe
it isn't worth so much, or forsake
the gleaming mind of Heidegger,

for a visit from just one whippoorwill
in these dead, unyielding barrens.
I heard the ache of its sobbing once
on my Acme crystal wireless set.
Its loneliness broke me, and in my mind
I could taste its bark-brown feathers.
Forgive me, old friend,
I've never felt so unfaithful.

Call me Coyote. My life in black outline
has been and will be eternal. Send
the trains, the red careening trucks,
speeding from the tunnel's one-way dark.
Flatten me under impossible boulders,
or calmly return my explosives
an instant before they explode,
I'll not relent. I'll live. I'll come for you.

My hunger erupts from someplace
much deeper than my belly. The nights
I wake in panic wet with sweat,
the growling I hear is outside my body.
A choir of my altered selves, twisted
and singing the anthem of my starvation,
in monstrous unison, their hymn to my gluttony,
loudly, from over the towering buttes.

I'll come for you again today refreshed,
with birdseed loaded with buckshot
and a magnet that could rip the very iron
from your blood. I'll grease my heels
and slide like light toward my prize,

unencumbered and missile-swift,
with dead-eye aim and avarice.

And patience, too, a patience so
unwavering it makes the mountains itch.
The creature in the sand awaits the canter
of your gait. The rock that watches you
watches you everywhere and knows
one day you will step upon the X
that marks the spot and spring the trap.

I'll take to the air today, perhaps,
in my pedal-powered whirlybird machine
to seed the clouds with silver iodine
and bring about a flood to wash
the sands completely clean of my fiascos,
a torrent you cannot outrun, a surge
of power so fierce you'll be swept,
finally – my greed, my gift, my life –
wet and gasping into my lean, ingenious arms.

When I want to be followed, my oversized feet
will leave rubberstamped tracks on the flat,
lime-bright, freshly painted forest floor.
When I want to be found, they will lead you
to the perfect black circle of my home,
where I'll appear to you and kiss you on the lips
to galvanize your bloodthirst, and then I'll tie
the double barrel of your shotgun in a bow.

Though I'm no man, I'm everyman, been everywhere.
I've tunnelled the world and made my den
in deserts, or high in the mountains of the west.
I've explored the frozen wastes, the restless seas,
and cheated death a dozen times, from the fires
of Hell to the chilling grip of far-flung space.
And still I find you, dogged hunter, stalking me,
optimistic, toffee-nosed, forgetful of the past.

Don't you remember? When I played the piano,
I had five fingers on each hand. I toured all Europe,
and still you followed, ever eager for my skin.
In the Venetian opera house, I bested you. Pansies
sprouted like pink children from your hairless,
gleaming crown, and you made for my neck,
cursing me: the bullet-dodger, the rascal!
Oh Elmer, your eyes! I'd thought you'd gone mad!

Should you come for me again, my friend,
take note: I am a master of disguise nonpareil,
and in my floral gown, in my headdress of fruit,

I will perform a slow, libidinous rumba for your
lonesome, aching heart, and in my dove-grey
three-piece suit with matching hat, I will rook you,
and leave you on a train bound for Alaska.
Oh, I know, I'm cruel, but you know I do it

out of love, don't you? When I tell you lies,
you believe them with all the credulity of a child
at vespers, like a little boy imploring the Lord
for a bike, or like the patient in the mental ward
who knows our lives, not his, are real and have flesh.
I do it because I love the sweetly girlish quality
of your cackle as a pair of muscular attendants
are tightening the buckles on your sleeves.

And though I almost know your thoughts before
you think them, and though you look ridiculous
in that hat, even I can take a wrong turn
at Albuquerque, even you could overwhelm me
with a spear and magic helmet, then carry my lifeless,
clobbered body, dolefully, into the darkened wings,
where I will no doubt find my feet, widen my eyes
and, with a little shrug, make a joke of happy endings.

The beauty of the striped hide
that hides the banded beast
in the bright and shaded grasses
never wants to die,
nor does the swiftness, triggered
by the noise of breath or steps
now reaching that vigilant heart,
that impels its body in a thought
far from the sharpened spear.

The business of killing things,
the hunter knows, is difficult
because of beauty and swiftness,
because his quarry astounds him
with its grace, and then it's gone.
Because nerve and hot breath
are inextricable, and strength
and stealth and pride all have their say.
He knows these things will not go quietly.

In preparation, he makes an image
on the wall and speaks the word.
There are other ways to capture things,
what they are and what they mean,
to hold them in the mind:
the beauty and swiftness of thoughts.
And now the sharpened spear
is ever sharper in the mind,
and swifter and more beautiful.

A change in the womb of light and the atomic
hourglass drains to zero. Barren. Expired.
When a star dies, the nova
briefly outshines the galaxy that bore it,

as though a firefly, fading, suddenly clicks
and fizzles, and its death levels a city.
As though the pin has been pulled from a grenade
that holds the sun. Next to anything so monstrous,

you and I are no different than a hermit thrush
and a hermit crab. A happy song and a helpless silence.
No different than a bustling hotel and a moon.
Every adjustment is a kind of violence. I take one

step and particles boil. You touch the door
and motion fails. Everything here is predictably
Newtonian. We attempt to shift together. We lean
into it. We move. But inertia has its foes.

CLOUD FORMATION LIKE A MAP OF THE WORLD

He's walking east toward your apartment,
and behind him the salmon-coloured sun
is only half an hour from turning scarlet.

He has the book you wanted. He's bringing you
the book, when high above him, between a pair
of tall buildings, a map of the world unfolds,

white outlines of the continents against the darkening
western sky, a blueprint for the planet unrolled
across the man-made table of commerce. A miracle?

No. He knows the life of miracles ended when
you left for the weekend and didn't return
for two months. When you finally came back,

you never looked at him the same way again.
Your eyes filled with miles of desert sand
and you slept. That was the end of miracles.

But now he's found the book you wanted,
the one filled with one man's love and art,
with New York City and statuary, and yes,

even miracles, at least the kind someone remembers
believing in, though now they've been refuted,
mauled by the passage of time, the savage

economics of collapse, the way that Africa
now dissolves into a shapeless mass as he walks
between the silver-plated towers of the debt collectors,

the way that Europe has been taffy-pulled
by invisible high-altitude winds into a long
white ribbon that resembles nothing anymore.

And now it's gone. Obliterated. No miracle at all,
just a trick of light and vapour. But he has the book
you wanted, its pages filled with emergencies and joy,

and not even the fleeting passing of the world,
its sudden destruction before his eyes,
will keep him from delivering it to you.

There are many ways to understand the word
lost, my love. When you were born, the last
Pyrenean ibex, a tawny female named Celia,
had not yet lived to see the view from Torla
overlooking Monte Perdido, but her great-
grandsire stood on the cliffs of Ordesa,
positioned on hoof-tips dainty as dimes,
and he shook his impregnable skull, a coffer
of brass and nobility crowned with bayonets,
as though in defiance of all who dwelt
in the highlands from Catalonia to Aquitaine.
Their kind is vanished now. Forever lost. *Perdido.*

And when you dressed in a Girl Guide's
uniform of Persian blue on Tuesday nights,
my love, in the long-lost basement of Grace
United Church, to play indoor baseball
and make believe that faerie magic
could make you rich or important or happy,
pods of baiji dolphins still swam in a river
you'd never heard of and would not think about
until years later, when together we would learn
from the evening news that the baiji
were lost, at last, from the Yangtze,
and in their place there came a universal emptiness.

There are many ways to understand the word
los⸱ ⸱t does not help to imagine a secret
⸱ lost things go. When last
ı ⸱ny arms, my love, the West

African black rhinoceros was still magnificent
and still alive, but now the gentleness of your breath
on my bare neck is as lost as the dusty, confident
snort of that once breathtaking beast. Great strength
is no protection, and neither is love. We are born,
and our births are lost. We can't go back to them.
Each embrace ends with an ending. When we become,
what we once thought we'd be is lost. We keep becoming.

NOTES

———

"Ape"
Koko is the best known of the gorillas residing at the Gorilla Foundation research centre in Woodside, California, where Dr. Francine "Penny" Patterson has taught her to communicate via GSL (Gorilla Sign Language, a slightly modified form of ASL that takes into account gorillas' relatively shorter thumbs, etc.). Koko has a vocabulary of approximately 1,000 signs, and she understands a further 2,000 words of spoken English.

Michael was Koko's companion; he also learned to sign. He was orphaned by bushmeat poachers in Cameroon when he was very young. In 1976, when Michael was three years old, he also came to live at the research centre in Woodside. When he was a full-grown silverback, researchers asked him what he remembered about his mother. His answer, "*Squash meat gorilla. Mouth tooth. Cry sharp-noise loud. Bad think-trouble look-face. Cut/neck lip (girl) hole*," is believed to be Michael's account of her death at the hands of the poachers. Michael died of heart failure in the year 2000 when he was only twenty-six years old.

"Dogstar"
Laika was the canine passenger aboard the Soviet satellite Sputnik 2, launched November 3, 1957. As such, she was the first living organism from Earth (larger than a microbe) to travel into space. Laika was never meant to return safely to Earth. Soviet scientists intended to poison her when she reached the end of her food supply to spare her the agony of burning up on re-entry. In actuality, Laika lived for only five to seven hours after takeoff. The life-support systems aboard the satellite failed, and Laika succumbed to heat exhaustion and stress. Sputnik 2 continued to orbit the Earth for 162 days.

"Elegy for Paul Winchell"
Winchell was an American ventriloquist, voice actor and inventor. As a ventriloquist, he is most famous for working with his dummies Jerry Mahoney and Knucklehead Smiff. As a voice actor, his credits are too numerous to mention, but perhaps most notably Winchell provided the voice for Tigger in Disney's Winnie-the-Pooh cartoons. As an inventor, Winchell held several patents, including one for a flameless cigarette lighter and another for the artificial heart. The latter he donated to the University of Utah where Robert Jarvik developed Winchell's prototype into the Jarvik 7 artificial heart.

"In Joseph Merrick's London"
Joseph Merrick was more popularly, and less humanely, known as the Elephant Man. For a long time, it was mistakenly thought that his first name was John. This is because Merrick's physician, Frederick Treves, misremembered Joseph's name in his memoirs. This simple error was repeated in almost all biographical material pertaining to Merrick for a century.

"Last of the Blondes"
In September 2002, major news outlets around the world announced that people with naturally blond hair would be extinct by the year 2202, citing a scientific study by the World Health Organization. The story was later revealed to be a hoax.

"The Reinvention of the Human Hand"
The failed attempts refer to the mouth-stick and service animals (dogs and monkeys) used by many quadriplegics. The "electric substitutes for nerves" refer to F.E.S. (functional electrical stimulation), an experimental medical treatment that has been shown to restore limited upper-body mobility to patients who were previously paralyzed from the neck down.

"The Sadness Will Last Forever"
It has been reported that Vincent Van Gogh's last words, spoken to
his brother Theo, were, "La tristesse durera toujours," which means,
"The sadness will last forever." Each stanza of this poem incorporates
a different quotation taken from the writings or reported speech of
Vincent Van Gogh.

"The Threatened Swan"
Jan Asselyn's painting *The Threatened Swan* (*circa* 1650) hangs in the
Rijksmuseum in Amsterdam. It depicts a swan defending her nest
from a prowling dog. Years after it was completed, an unknown vandal
painted political slogans into the painting. The woman who inspired
this poem is real. As far as I know, her children are safe.

"Twenty-one Days with a Baboon Heart"
"Baby Fae" was the name the media used to refer to Fae Traphagan,
a newborn who received an experimental xenotransplant of a baboon
heart (the first of its kind) in 1984, after which she lived for only
twenty-one days.

ACKNOWLEDGEMENTS

I am grateful for the financial support of the Toronto Arts Council, the Ontario Arts Council and the Canada Council for the Arts.

I am especially grateful to Ellen Seligman, Anita Chong and everyone at McClelland & Stewart who made this book possible.

Many thanks once again to Albert Moritz, whose keen editorial eye helped to shape this book.

Many of these poems benefited from the scrutiny and wisdom of friends. Thanks to Marianne Apostolides, Chris Banks, Evie Christie, Jeff Latosik, Jacob McArthur Mooney, George Murray, Stuart Ross, Alysia Shewchuk, Chris Sloan, Bob Stewart, Nick Thran, Silas White, Carleton Wilson, Patrick Woodcock and Mary-Lou Zeitoun.

Thanks also to Dionne Brand and my classmates in the University of Guelph MFA in creative writing.

Some of these poems have appeared previously, often as earlier versions. Thanks are due to the editors of the following periodicals: *The Delinquent* (UK), *Event Magazine*, *Exile: The Literary Quarterly*, *Eye Weekly*, the *Globe and Mail*, *Matrix Magazine*, *Misunderstandings Magazine*, *New American Writing* (USA), *Pax Americana* (USA), *Queen Street Quarterly*, *Rampike*, *Taddle Creek*, *This Magazine* and *The Walrus*.

Some poems have also appeared on www.northernpoetryreview.com and on the Canadian Parliamentary Poet Laureate's *Poem of the Week* website, as part of the Spire Poetry Poster Series, and in the anthology *VERSschmuggel / ReVERSible (Canadian Poetry – Poesie du Quebec)* produced in Germany by the Berlin Poetry Festival, the Literaturwerkstatt and Verlag das Wunderhorn, and co-published in Canada by Les Éditions du Noroît of Quebec.

The epigraph at the front of this book is taken from the essay "Thingitude and Causality: In Praise of Materialism" by Tony Hoagland. It is collected in his book *Real Sofistikashun: Essays on Poetry and Craft*, published by Graywolf Press in 2006.